MESSAGES OF

MESSAGES OF ....

365 DAYS

OF INSPIRATION
& MOTIVATION

A Motivational Quote A Day For
Increased Joy, Happiness And
Success

Kay Sanders

Messages Of Inspiration

365 Days of Inspiration and Motivation

A Motivational Quote A Day For Increased Joy, Happiness And Success

Kay Sanders Coaching
www.kaysanders.com

ISBN: 1985667754
ISBN-13: 978-1985667754

DEDICATION

I dedicate this book to my parents Rosie and Peter Gerlach, to my son Darian, and to my friends and fellow entrepreneurs Dale Darley and Eva Lukacs who have been so supportive on my journey of discovering myself, and finding my true purpose in life. I am very grateful to have you all by my side.

MESSAGES OF INSPIRATION

CONTENTS

MESSAGES OF INSPIRATION

ACKNOWLEDGMENTS

I would like to acknowledge **you** for your tenacity, your dedication, your willingness to change your thinking, to shift your beliefs, to make a difference in your own life and the life of others and going after what your heart desires.

I also would like to acknowledge all the change makers who are out there making a difference in the world, who have taken their own challenges, adversities and difficulties they have experienced to lead the way to bring hope, guidance and change to those in need.

MESSAGES OF INSPIRATION

CHAPTER ONE

INTRODUCTION

Could you use some light in your life, some motivation to go after your dreams? Some inspiration to help you stay focused and in awe of what is truly possible for you?

We often forget that we are infinite beings, who can do, be and have anything our heart desires but we often get derailed by our negative and limiting thoughts, the illusions we live by that keeps us playing small because we fear change, we fear failure, or we simply don't think more is in store for us.

If this sounds familiar then these 365 days of inspiration and motivation will bring back the light that has been missing in your life. These messages come directly from the Universe and the Beings of Light that wanted me to share these messages with you to inspire you, that you truly are an infinite being, that you do deserve all the greatness you desire and also to shine that light into your life that has been keeping you disconnected from what is truly possible for you.

Each message holds a deeper meaning for you that only you can decipher for yourself. They are messages that only you will understand the true meaning of each word. These messages will shine light onto the challenges you have been facing as well as guide you on setting yourself free from those negative patterns, the gremlins that have been holding you back from stepping into your full potential and going after your dreams and what your heart desires.

On my search for more joy, happiness, success as well as fulfillment, I have learned different modalities but one has been most profound and truly changed my life, which is also what lead me to bring these 365 quotes of inspiration and motivation to you; which is accessing the Akashic Records. As I was asking for guidance about certain areas in my own life, I received the spiritual guidance to share these messages with the world and this is how these 365 messages came about; to bring you divine guidance from the Universe.

If you are at a point in your life where you are ready to step outside of your bubble, to claim what you truly desire, then these quotes will help you stay motivated and inspired to take that next step onto your journey of great joy, happiness, and success.

I promise that these messages will bring you great joy, inspiration, and motivation to tackle each day and to help you stay on your path to never giving up, to keep moving forward and going after your dreams and creating the life your heart desires. These quotes have brought me great inspiration and motivation especially on days that I felt disconnected, overwhelmed and even stressed. These messages brought me back to reality, reminding me that I am a divine being, that I am capable of creating the life of my dreams; and you are no different. You too are a divine being with infinite possibilities and the ability to create the life of your dreams.

If you have had that longing to be, do and have more then don't wait! Don't be that person who envies others for all that they have, for the great lifestyle they live, for the amazing success they experience, for the joy and happiness they radiate. You too can create this lifestyle for yourself; believe that anything is possible for you, that you too can have all that your heart desires.

Abundance, joy, happiness and great success is not something that is reserved for others; you too can create all the abundance, all the joy, all the happiness and all the success your heart desires. Be the person who does not let their situation or circumstance determine their life. You can choose to say NO to all the struggles, say NO to the challenges you may be experiencing and say YES to abundance, say YES to Joy, Happiness and immense Success in your life.

The messages you will find within these 365 days of inspiration and motivation are divine messages that will bring you the inspiration and motivation to help you stay your course towards creating the life you desire, to create more joy, happiness, and success in your life.

If you are ready to be inspired and motivated to change your life, to change your thinking and to create more joy, happiness, and success in your life than visit **www.MessagesOfInspiration.com** to request the accompanying daily email series and keep on reading.

CHAPTER TWO

HOW TO USE THIS BOOK

This book is designed to be used in different ways. You could read the messages one day at a time, reflect on each message, and journal about what comes up for you.

You could also read the book as slow or as fast as you like, or go back to these messages whenever you need that extra boost of inspiration and motivation.

However, the best way to use this book, and to get the most out of these messages is to opt-in to receive these messages in the form of daily emails which also come with additional action steps for you to take each day. To request the accompanying daily emails visit **www.MessagesOfInspiration.com**.

By focusing on one message a day, tuning into the message, journaling about what comes up for you when tuning into the message, and completing the daily action steps you will receive in your email, you will get the most benefit out of these messages.

Take the time to reflect on each message, don't just read through and move on, really take the time to tune into each of the messages as each message has a specific meaning that applies to you in this moment, when you re-read the same message a few month later, it might have a different meaning and a different underlying message that applies to you in that moment.

However, these messages are designed to bring change, to inspire and to motivate but you do have to be open to receiving the deeper meaning of each message and take inspired actions based on the guidance, or inspiration, you receive by tuning into each of these messages. You alone know the meaning, these messages are simply the guide that points you in the right direction.

Request the daily email series!
www.MessagesOfInspiration.com

CHAPTER THREE

365 INSPIRATIONAL AND MOTIVATIONAL QUOTES

Set foot on your path and keep moving forward with
your desired destination in mind.

Nothing is as difficult as it may seem. Re-evaluate
your current situation and ask yourself does this still
serve you, is there anything that you can let go of in
order to break free from those challenges you are
facing. Get clarity on what you desire to create in your
life and take inspired actions.

Take action out of inspiration, not desperation. When
you are in the flow of inspiration, abundance will
manifest in greater forms.

Envision your future as the dream you would like to have enfold. Stay within the vibration and visualize as it is already your reality.

Your message is meant to be heard, do not hide your gifts, your message, or yourself behind the illusions that your message is not worth sharing.

There are infinite possibilities for each and every one.

Stay within your power, don't allow your fear to derail you; you alone have the power to create the life you desire.

Forward movement requires going within. Lay out the map of your desired destination and follow your inner map by taking inspired action and trust that you are divinely guided.

You alone determine your destiny, the actions you take, the inactions you take, the thoughts you choose, the beliefs you choose. Be in alignment with your beliefs, your thoughts and your actions and trust that you are divinely guided on your path to creating your destiny.

Learn the tools that are needed to move forward on your path. Implement the things you learn as you go along, do not allow yourself to learn without taking the necessary actions to implement what you have learned.

All the answers you seek are within you. Ask and listen to the silent whisper of your soul providing you the answers you are looking for.

See the beauty that is all around you, even in moments where all you think you can see is overwhelm, frustration or lack. In moments like these look around and see all the beautiful things around you and in your life.

Abundance starts within your heart. Feel your desire within, not only think about what you want but pull it into your heart and feel the emotion that is in alignment with what your heart desires.

———— ⁓⚬⚬⁓ ————

Take time to yourself; there is nothing more important than taking care of yourself, your physical self as well as your divine self. Both need to be nurtured and well taken care of in order to shine your light brightly and make the difference in the world.

———— ⁓⚬⚬⁓ ————

Rest and rejuvenation are just as important as taking action. Refuel your body, mind, and soul in order to feel refreshed to take the necessary actions.

———— ⁓⚬⚬⁓ ————

You have the power to create the life you desire. If you desire more opportunities believe that they are available to you, open yourself up to receive all that is available to you, release your hold and attachment to the outcome. Surrender!

———— ⁓⚬⚬⁓ ————

If you feel lonesome on your entrepreneurial island, find like-minded entrepreneurs, build your own community and you will no longer feel alone.

———

Take time to reflect on all you have accomplished up until this present moment. Acknowledge yourself for your accomplishments, your dedication, and forward movement.

———

Be OK with where you are, as you are right where you are meant to be! All happens in divine timing!

———

Take time to just be! Put aside the busyness of "doing" and focus on "being" in the moment, being present, being your true divine self.

———

Find joy in every moment, live to the fullest and allow your inner light to shine brightly. Only when you are in alignment with yourself, stay within a place of love and joy, magic will start to happen your life will overflow with joy, happiness, and abundance.

———

There are many paths that can lead you to your desired destination if you are unsure of which path to go on, go within and make a decision based on what you feel within your heart rather than what you think is best for you. Follow your intuition and allow yourself to be guided.

Blessings are on its way, even if you may not see them at this given moment. You are always supported to the degree you allow yourself to be supported. If you desire more money, more opportunities or other things, increase your allowing to receive all that you desire.

All your efforts and dedication will pay off in due time. Stay on your path and believe that all is possible.

Anything you desire to manifest is created from within. Envision what you desire, feel as if you already have what you desire, believe that it is possible and trust that it is on its way.

Every day is a new day, a new opportunity to make a difference, to get one step closer to reaching for your dreams.

Progress means taking consistent action, one step at a time, towards a desired goal.

How do you achieve anything in life? You take it one step at a time.

The key to an amazing day is to make it an intention to have an amazing day!

Consistency is what makes the difference. Anything in life can be achieved if you take consistent action and consistently work towards your goals, one step at a time.

In order to get what we want, we must know exactly what it is we want and why we want it.

Struggling is not a sign of failure, it's a sign that you are on the right track.

The hardest part of experiencing a "failure" or "something not working out" is not to take it personal because everything in life, every failure, every challenge, every "it didn't work out" holds a gift and a lesson you are meant to learn.

Manifestation and Abundance starts with gratitude for the things you already have in life.

Your future is not determined by your past or past failures. You have the power to create the future you desire. You are the creator of your destiny!

Big goals are not achieved all at once, they require multiple smaller goals that lead up to the big goal.

Dream Big. Set Goals. Ask for what you want. Have Faith that it will come, and be open to Receive!

Our past failures are not what determines our future; they are lessons we were meant to learn in order to be taken on the path we were meant to be on.

Everything has a beginning and an end but all that matters is the now!

What can you do "now" to make a difference in your life? What can you do "now" that will get you one step closer to reaching your goals and dreams? What can you do "now" to make yourself and others happy?

Sometimes the most unexpected things happen in the most unexpected ways.

Being able to manifest what we most desire starts within. How we feel inside reflect outside. You can't manifest or attract abundance if you have a lack mindset.

———

Success is made up of 90% inner work and 10% outer work.

———

If you can dream about your dream life, your perfect day, the things you want to accomplish in life then you can make these dreams a reality. Claim the life you desire and make it your reality!

———

When opportunity knocks, do you usually answer or just peek through the window and debate if you should open the door and invite it in?

———

Once you find pure joy and fulfillment in what you do, and your actions are driven by passion, joy and the drive to feel fulfilled, will you be able to create great abundance in all areas of your life.

———

Vibrating on the frequency of allowing, is the essence of attracting great abundance into your life.

———

Do not judge yourself or be hard on yourself as you have already come a long way and you are heading in the right direction.

———

Act out of inspiration rather than fear, as actions taken out of fear or worry will not bring you the satisfaction and abundance you desire. Whereas when you take action out of joy and inspiration you are opening the doors for great abundance to enter into your life.

———

Joy and gratitude is a vital piece of abundance, only when you feel joy and gratitude within your heart, more abundance will flow to you. Be grateful for all that you have, act from a place of joy as this tells the universe you desire more of what you already have to come to you in even greater abundance.

———

Happiness does not come from the place you live in, the home you have, the car you drive, or how much money you have in the bank. Happiness comes from within. You alone know what it means to be and feel happy. No outside source can make you happy, you alone can make yourself happy by feeling happy within.

Follow your heart as it will lead you on your path. Tune out those who attempt to derail you, trust in yourself and stay on your path as it will lead you to greater happiness and abundance.

All of your efforts will be rewarded whenever the time is right but know that all you do today is part of your journey and even if you don't see the rewards right away, it will come in divine timing. Keep moving forward and know you are divinely guided.

Release your self-doubt as you are magnificent and a divine being. Look back at how far you have come, be proud of who you are and all that you have accomplished in life.

You can create your dream life wherever you are right now. All it takes is to set the intention to create and live your dream life… right now and right here!

———

It is you who creates the life of your dreams, the circumstances in your life, the experiences you have. But it starts within your heart. Let go of the material things or requirements in your life, this is not what brings you happiness, you alone have the power to create happiness in your life by how you feel each and every day.

———

If you are filled with love, joy, and happiness, then this is what you will attract more of into your life.

———

When you are in a place of love and truth, and see yourself as being part of the whole, being one with all, then there is no room for judgment, hate, frustration, blame, or anger. In every situation, you have a choice how you respond. You can choose to respond in anger, frustration, or hate or you can respond in love and understanding.

———

In order to manifest your heart's desire, be kind, love yourself and others, and enter each day filled with love and joy. See the beauty in each day, in each moment, and be present in the now. Let go of the past, let go of the worries about the future, be here in the moment because the now is all you have. The now is all that is important.

———— ～∽ⵚⵛ∽～ ————

To heal yourself, love yourself, forgive yourself and know that all that happened in your past was to your highest good that lead you on your path.

———— ～∽ⵚⵛ∽～ ————

Allow yourself to let go of all that no longer serves you, let go of the hurt, the pain, the agony, as it is all within. No one can hurt you unless you allow it, no one can take your power away unless you give your power away, you cannot fail unless you allow it. All comes from within! Your outer world is a mirror reflection of what is going on within yourself.

———— ～∽ⵚⵛ∽～ ————

We live in our self-made prison which hinders us from experience the infinite possibilities for joy, happiness and immense wealth and success. By setting yourself free from your inner gremlins, you break down the walls of your self-made prison that is to keep you safe within your comfort zone but also far away from experiencing immense joy in your life.

If you can envision what you desire with your mind's eye then you can create it.

In order to create a breakthrough in your life, see yourself as if you have already accomplished what you desire, ask yourself what would it mean for you to achieve this breakthrough. Give yourself permission to feel this breakthrough in this given moment.

The current moment is all that matters as you create your experience in every moment. If you allow yourself to feel this breakthrough in each moment then you ultimately create this breakthrough for yourself in every given moment.

The power is within you to create anything your heart
desires. You simply need to step into your power,
step into your purpose and see yourself worthy and
deserving. See yourself as the amazing being that you
are.

During challenging times, know that these challenges
bring you the greatest gifts and opportunities to grow.

You are an amazing being that deep down knows no
limitations. You alone give yourself limitations due to
fear, and lack of trust in yourself. But know that you
hold the power to shift things around and you can tap
into the infinite power you hold within, and you can
create the life you so deeply desire. It is all within you!

Go within, find that light, find the passion you have
buried deep inside. Amplify your brightness and make
your inner light shine brighter and brighter. Let the
light consume you from the inside out and focus on
that light, that passion, that hunger, the deep desire to
make a difference and go after what you desire.

The universe has many ways of giving you the life you want and even better than you can imagine. Just allow yourself to be open to the possibilities, the opportunities; be open to whatever comes your way and listen to your intuition as it will guide you along the way.

———————— ∞ ————————

You have magic in your life, you are more than capable to create and manifest anything your heart desires but it all starts within. You manifest from the inside out, not from the outside in.

———————— ∞ ————————

You must feel deserving of what you desire, you must feel worthy of receiving, you must appreciate what you already have in your life, what you have accomplished…. Only then will you be able to receive more of what you desire.

———————— ∞ ————————

The answer you are looking for lies within. Quite your mind, go within and the answers you are looking for will reveal themselves to you

———————— ∞ ————————

All the abundance you seek is already here, all the money you desire, all the joy and happiness, all is already here. Open yourself up to receiving the infinite abundance and prosperity and you will see it all. All will be revealed to you as soon as you are ready to see.

———————— ⬥ ————————

Envision the person you desire to be, embody this vision with every breath you take, every move you make, every action you take. Embody this vision in every waking moment.

———————— ⬥ ————————

The only person depriving you of what you desire is you. Step away and separate yourself from your ego mind which is trying to keep you safe by hindering you from going after what you desire. Say NO to the struggle, say NO to settling, and allow yourself to receive all that your heart desires.

———————— ⬥ ————————

Abundance is all around you, open your eyes to the fast beauty and abundance available to you in this and every moment. When you see and feel abundance more will come.

———————— ⬥ ————————

The beauty of stepping into your true purpose is that it fulfills you in every cell of your body, it brings you joy that you will feel deep within your core.

───────

Make joy part of your everyday life as it is the essence to great happiness, fulfillment, and abundance.

───────

All the abundance you seek is already there, all the money you desire, all the love and joy, all the happiness you desire, all is already available to you. Open your eyes and heart to the infinite abundance and prosperity and all will be revealed to you.

───────

The lessons we are meant to learn are taught to us by the teachers who are meant to guide us on our path.

───────

Your thoughts are attached to an emotion and the emotion of your thought is the energy that brings you more of what you think about.

───────

Love and gratitude is the essence to manifesting great abundance and prosperity.

Open up to love, trust and have faith that you are on the right path.

Watch your thoughts as what you think about will come about. If you desire abundance, joy, happiness, and success then focus on thoughts that are in alignment with these emotions.

Financial abundance is manifested by doing something that brings you joy. Anything you do that brings you anything other than joy closes the doors to financial abundance.

Each day be in harmony with your desire. Envision, feel and embody the very thing you desire to manifest into your life.

Align yourself with the success you desire to achieve, the abundance you desire to create, and the freedom you desire to experience. Any thoughts and feelings that are not in alignment with what you desire to create will derail your efforts.

———

Stay on your path, do not lose hope or allow others to derail you from moving towards your desired destination. Keep moving forward as all you desire is already there for you, waiting for you to claim it.

———

Be open to love, be open to possibility, be open to joy, be open to receive all that you are asking for.

———

Focus on the NOW! All that matters is the here and now. Nothing that happened in the past matters in the NOW, nothing that is going to happen tomorrow or in the future matters in the NOW. All that matters is this present moment!

———

Nothing good will come from worrying about the future, or dwelling on the past. You can't change the past, you can't predict the future, all you can do is be present in the moment and stay in alignment with who you truly are.

―――――

Don't give into worry, fear, frustration or anger as it no longer serves you. Free yourself from the negativity and fill your heart with love and light.

―――――

Being in a state of gratitude will diminish any fears, any worries or doubts as gratitude is light and fear is darkness. There is no darkness where there is light.

―――――

All it takes is a second to shift your thinking, to shift your emotional state, to shift from negative emotions into gratitude and being present in the moment without dwelling on the past or worrying about the future.

―――――

When you stay in the NOW, focus on the good, the beauty in life, and focus on gratitude, you then shift into positive vibration which will then open up the gates to abundance and prosperity.

———— ⟶ ❈ ⟵ ————

You have unlimited power to create the life you desire. Raise your vibration, as this is where you will find the freedom you so desire.

———— ⟶ ❈ ⟵ ————

When you open your heart, raise your vibration, and focus on empowering and positive thoughts you will shift into allowing infinite possibilities which are always right in front of you.

———— ⟶ ❈ ⟵ ————

Be open to the possibilities of experiencing true love. Love that knows no bounds, love that fills every inch of your being, love that fulfills you. Because this is the only love you deserve.

———— ⟶ ❈ ⟵ ————

All of your past actions have planted the seeds which will soon be starting to bloom and bring you great joy, happiness, and success.

———

Manifesting can happen in an instant if you are ready to receive what you desire.

———

If you want to manifest financial abundance, ask yourself, who do you need to become in order to allow financial abundance?

———

Accept that there will be setbacks but know that these setbacks are for your highest and greatest good as they hold many gifts, and lessons to be learned to help you become who you are meant to become.

———

If you wish to attract greater abundance, then let go of the worries and fears. Instead, focus on the opportunities and infinite possibilities of abundance available to you.

———

In order to create the future you are destined to have, you must first let go of the past. Any negative feelings you are holding on to are only holding you back from stepping into your true purpose and keeping you from becoming who you are meant to become.

In order to create the future you are destined to have, you must first let go of the past. Any negative feelings you are holding on to are only holding you back from stepping into your true purpose and keeping you from becoming who you are meant to become.

Let go of your fears, your worries, your doubts and past experiences which no longer serve you in order to change your life.

Believe that what you desire is truly possible for you. Without belief there is no trust, without trust is no believing.

Set clear boundaries and be clear on what you are willing to tolerate and what is not acceptable. Never lower your standards to please others. Never be anything less than who you truly are within.

Decide on who you want to be, what you want to have, what you want to do. Claim it and Own it!

Your outer world is a mirror reflection of your inner world. If you are dissatisfied with your outer experiences, ask yourself where do I experience this within? To change your experience, change your thinking and feelings.

———

There is a reason behind every action and every inaction.

———

Your ego is the part of you that is trying to protect you, trying to keep you save. When you trust and love yourself deeply, will you be able to tune out the negative chatter from your ego mind.

———

Limitations are meant to help you grow as you find a way to break through the limitations you set for yourself.

———

Limitations are illusions we tell ourselves in order to keep ourselves safe within our comfort zone.

———

Do not fear change, instead embrace it. Only when you embrace change, welcome and nurture it, will you be able to set yourself free from the fears that hold you back, that keeps you playing small.

Treat each day as a new beginning, a clean slate from the old, the happenings of the day prior. Each day you can choose a different route that will lead you to your desired destination.

You are connected to the creator of all things, to source, to the divine. Nurture this connection by going within, quieting your ego mind in order to receive divine guidance to help you co-create with the creator of all things and manifest your heart's desire.

Make joy a part of your everyday life as it is the essence of great happiness, fulfillment, and abundance.

Circumstances do not define our life. How we react to these circumstances define the outcome.

———— ·ᘓᗴᘓ· ————

Every new day gives you the opportunity to leave your past behind. It gives you the opportunity to choose differently, and make choices that are in alignment with your true self, in alignment with who you are meant to become.

———— ·ᘓᗴᘓ· ————

Have a clear vision of the life you desire, the things you desire to have, who you desire to be, and what you desire to do. Hold on to that vision and each day take inspired action that will lead you towards what you desire.

———— ·ᘓᗴᘓ· ————

Remove the mask of fear, of worry, of struggle, and come forth from behind that mask you have been hiding behind. Shine your light brightly, show the world who you are without that mask.

———— ·ᘓᗴᘓ· ————

The agony and despair of the past are in the past. Release yourself from the negative experience and set yourself free from the shackles of the past that have been holding you back, that have been keeping you imprisoned from going after what you desire. Set yourself free once and for all!

———— ·ᗱᗴᑢᗴ· ————

Find your voice, share your message, do not fear to speak your truth as this is who you truly are.

———— ·ᗱᗴᑢᗴ· ————

Surrender your desires, surrender your wishes, let go of the "need to know the how" as the answers to your questions will be revealed to you once you let go of the control.

———— ·ᗱᗴᑢᗴ· ————

Co-creation with the divine, with source, with the creator of all, happens when you surrender your desires and allow divine guidance to guide you on your way.

———— ·ᗱᗴᑢᗴ· ————

All that happens, happens for a reason, it happens in divine timing, for your highest and greatest good.

———— ·ᗱᗴᑢᗴ· ————

You don't need to make anyone happy other than yourself. Your own happiness is all that matters. No one can give you what you need but yourself.

———

Open yourself up to the infinite possibilities, the infinite opportunities available to you.

———

Self-love is the key to filling the void you may experience. When you love yourself unconditionally, nothing is missing, all is well.

———

Your confidence, or lack of such, is the mirror reflection of your self-worth and self-love. When you know your worth and love yourself deeply, you will radiate an immense confidence that will not go unnoticed.

———

Believe in yourself as you are a divine being that is right where you are supposed to be.

———

Success, wealth, and prosperity are not achieved by the amount of action you take, rather than who you need to become that allows these things to manifest into your life.

―――――――――― ⋯⋯ ⋅⋅⋅ ――――――――

Abundance and prosperity is not something you create, it is something you allow and become.

―――――――――― ⋯⋯ ⋅⋅⋅ ――――――――

Your beliefs are the driving force that determines your feelings, your actions and inactions.

―――――――――― ⋯⋯ ⋅⋅⋅ ――――――――

The choices we make create our circumstances.

―――――――――― ⋯⋯ ⋅⋅⋅ ――――――――

Take responsibility for your actions and choices you make in order to change your circumstances.

―――――――――― ⋯⋯ ⋅⋅⋅ ――――――――

We alone create the life we live and the circumstances we experience because we made conscious or unconscious choices that led us to where we are in this moment.

―――――――――― ⋯⋯ ⋅⋅⋅ ――――――――

You can create the life you desire by making choices that are in alignment with the life you desire to create for yourself.

———— ⁓∾⊗∾⁓ ————

The negative and limiting mind chatter is your egos way of keeping you distracted from going after what you truly want.

———— ⁓∾⊗∾⁓ ————

You have the power to create all that you desire. Trust in that power and release the fear and worries that are keeping you from stepping into and embodying this power to create and manifest all that you desire.

———— ⁓∾⊗∾⁓ ————

New beginnings are part of life; welcome a new beginning as this gives you the opportunity to leave all the old, the negative, the things that no longer serve you behind. Embody a new powerful you that is no longer driven by the past.

———— ⁓∾⊗∾⁓ ————

Dark times come and go… shine your light to make the darkness go away. Focus on the beauty in your life, find something to be grateful for and you will bring back the light.

———————

Fill your heart with love whenever you feel lonesome.

———————

To create love in your life, feel love within your heart. To create freedom, feel free within. To create abundance, feel abundant. All you desire to create in your life, you create within you first.

———————

Believe that money wants to come to you, know that there is always more available to you.

———————

Be conscious of your reactions to and about money as it will determine your effortlessness to manifest more.

———————

The past only repeats itself if you allow it to, by not allowing yourself to let go of the past.

———————

You can choose a different outcome by making choices and taking actions that are based on what you desire instead of fear and worries.

Notice your thoughts and actions which are not in alignment and make the conscious decision to choose differently, to come from a place of joy and abundance.

Let go of the feeling of obligation as it will only bring you circumstances of more obligation. Each moment choose you! When you choose you first, there is no obligation, all that is, is you and what you desire for yourself.

All of your experiences both good and bad come from your thoughts and feelings. To have more good experiences, choose thoughts and feelings that represent good circumstances and experiences.

You always have the power to choose differently. No one can force you into thinking, feeling or behaving a certain way; you alone make the choice in each moment of your life.

————— ⌘ —————

Your actions are determined by the choices you make both consciously and unconsciously.

————— ⌘ —————

Your success, your financial wealth, your entire life is a mirror reflection of your self-worth and the level of feeling deserving. If you desire more success, more wealth, and more abundance in your life, increase your self-worth and feeling of deserving.

————— ⌘ —————

Blocks, obstacles, and challenges are created in your mind first, the doubt that you can't achieve certain tasks, the worry that It may be difficult, the fear that you may fail. All these are illusions that are created in your mind. Believe in yourself, trust that you are more than capable, and know that there are no failures only opportunities to grow. Set yourself free from the illusions, the lies that you call blocks, challenges, and obstacles.

————— ⌘ —————

Each day choose joy and satisfaction over obligation
and the need to do certain things.

———— ❦ ————

You create freedom by choosing to be free and not
settling for anything less than the freedom you desire.

———— ❦ ————

Settling for less is an act of devaluing your divine
worth. By choosing less than what your heart desires
you lose yourself in the illusions that this is all there is
instead of raising the bar, standing for and demanding
what you truly want. Because you are divine, you
deserve all that you desire and even more. Never
settle!

———— ❦ ————

We each are responsible for our own happiness; no
one else can bring us the happiness we desire. If you
are looking for happiness, start by looking within,
what can you do today to create more happiness in
your life? Don't wait for others, take responsibility
and create your happiness in whatever way you desire.
Because you can!

———— ❦ ————

The thing you may fear the most is who you will become once you step into your purpose, once you step outside of your comfort zone and embrace who you are within.

———— ⋆⋅☼⋅⋆ ————

The beauty of this world is all around you. You can see this vast beauty even through all the darkness if you are willing to find the beautiful things that are all around you.

———— ⋆⋅☼⋅⋆ ————

Embrace the things you fear, that make you uncomfortable, as these will bring you the biggest, most amazing growth and opportunities.

———— ⋆⋅☼⋅⋆ ————

Any limiting beliefs you have are learned beliefs which can be unlearned and replaced with empowering beliefs.

———— ⋆⋅☼⋅⋆ ————

Life is a journey full of wonders, opportunities, adventures, and excitement. It is up to you to say YES to the journey that will lead you on your path towards your life's purpose. If you decide to say NO, you will stay in a place of wonder, a place of longing for more, a longing for fulfillment. So say YES to life, say YES to the journey and prepare yourself for a wild ride!

You hold the answers to all your questions and desires in your heart. Open yourself up for your inner guidance as you already know your next steps towards your desires.

The teachers that come into your life are meant to provide you with different opportunities to learn valuable life lessons or to redirect you into the right direction that lead you onto your path.

Stay your path even if your future seems unsure and all your efforts seem they don't bare any fruits, keep moving forward as you soon will see your life unfold.

Be open to the many lessons life wants to teach you. All lessons learned are valuable and hold a gift and even if you may not see it in the moment, but all that happens, happens for you and for your highest and greatest good.

———

Life is a book of many chapters, where each chapter leads into the next, where each chapter reveals more of your life path. Step back and view your life as such, where you are the author of your story.

———

You know you are on purpose when your heart sings when you feel uplifted by your life, by the things you do and every moment brings you great joy.

———

In order to find your purpose, you must ask yourself, what brings you the most joy? What does your heart long for? What fills that emptiness within? Once you have found the answers, you have found your purpose.

———

Purpose comes from your personal experiences, it is the things you have struggled with most and learned how to break free from. It is these life lessons that lead you on your path to discovering your true purpose.

In order to receive greater abundance in your life, be willing to receive abundance in all areas of your life not only financial abundance but also an abundance of health, relationships, love, freedom, and vitality.

The stillness within is where all your answers, your desires, your wants reside. To get the answers you are looking for, go within, quite your mind and the answers will reveal themselves to you.

Love is about being one with yourself. Loving yourself unconditionally first before you are able to give and receive unconditional love.

We are all one! One with the divine, one with source, once with everyone and everything around us. Remember this oneness anytime you feel alone.

———— ⟊ ————

There is always light at the end of the tunnel. Even in situations that seem hopeless or too challenging with no way out. Know that there is light, your efforts will pay off, no situation is too difficult for you to handle.

———— ⟊ ————

To find your true passion, allow yourself to discover what brings you most joy and fulfillment. The very thing that makes your heart sing, is what your soul longs for. By uncovering your passion you will be one step closer to becoming one with your true self.

———— ⟊ ————

Any situation you are facing holds a gift and a valuable lesson. Both, good and bad situations are meant to either teach you something or deliver a message with a deeper meaning. Be open to receiving these messages as they are part of your journey.

———— ⟊ ————

Honor your wishes, your desires and wants. Don't allow others to dismiss what you desire as you are the only person that is responsible for your happiness, joy, and success. Just as everyone else is responsible for their own happiness, joy, and success.

———

Your dream life isn't created in a day, but your vision of your dream life can be created within an instant. Once you have that mental image, hold on to that image and start creating your dream life from the inside out.

———

Anytime you experience a challenge take a step back to evaluate your willingness to being guided by your intuition. If you experience a challenge you may have allowed your ego mind to be in control rather than listening to your inner guidance system which is trying to lead the way.

———

Refrain from chasing after your dreams; instead, allow yourself to be in the flow of allowing greatness to enter into your life.

———

Nothing you chase after is worth the effort. Anything that is meant to be in your life will appear in divine timing and as soon as you allow it. No chasing is necessary as all you desire is available to you... if you allow it.

Your level of self-love is reflected back to you by the people that are close to you.

Don't be afraid to demand what you desire, you deserve all the greatness and abundance you wish for. There is abundance everywhere; you never have to settle for less.

People enter your life at a time that is to your highest and greatest good, but they also leave your life at a point in time that is to your highest and greatest good.

Love and forgiveness is the key to great joy and happiness in life. Where there is love there cannot be hate. Where there is light there cannot be darkness.

Satisfaction in life is achieved by doing something you love, something that excites you, something that puts a smile on your face and leaves you in awe of how amazing you feel, how complete you feel as a divine being.

―――――――――――

Allow yourself to forgive those who have hurt you in the past, forgive yourself for any hurt you have caused yourself or others. Step away from the shadows of hate and blame and step into love and forgiveness. This is the essence of creating more joy and happiness in your life.

―――――――――――

The past is a part of your life's journey but you alone are responsible for either allowing your past to keep a hold on you or to let go of the past as the past no longer matters. All that matters is the here and now.

―――――――――――

Release the darkness of the past by focusing on the here and now. Replace the past by the vision of a greater, more joyful future.

―――――――――――

The past may be influencing you in the now but you can influence the future by making choices in the now that are in alignment with your future vision rather than your past pains and disappointments.

———

Your reality can be influenced and changed just like a situation in your dream. Rewrite the story of your life like you would rewrite the story of your dream.

———

Every situation can be perceived in a positive light or in a negative light. The outcome depends on your perception of the situation. Change your perception; change the outcome.

———

If you desire more success, become that person which allows more success. If you desire more joy and happiness, become that person who allows more joy and happiness.

———

If your allowing is not in alignment with what you desire, then increase your allowing, give yourself the permission to be open to receiving all that you desire, right now and right here.

———————— ⟨⟩ ————————

If you desire more in your life ask yourself where do you feel lack? More does not always replace the lack you feel, it may just be a way of trying to fill an emptiness in your heart.

———————— ⟨⟩ ————————

Abundance is not achieved by acquiring more material things or wealth, abundance is acquired by feeling abundant within.

———————— ⟨⟩ ————————

A healthy body is necessary to have a healthy mind. Without the body there is no mind. If the body is not healthy, nurtured and well taken care of, the mind will suffer from the neglect.

———————— ⟨⟩ ————————

Your story is all it is, a story you tell yourself to either talk yourself into taking a certain action or out of taking a certain action all with the intention of keeping you safely within your comfort zone.

When you fear change you must get uncomfortable with being comfortable. Only when you are uncomfortable with the comfort you feel by staying safe, will you be tenacious enough to get comfortable with change.

Excuses are the illusions that drive our actions. If the actions you take are not in alignment with moving towards your desired goals then it may be the illusions you keep telling yourself why you can't have what you want, why you may not be good enough or that it's simply not in the cards for you, that is causing you to take the wrong actions or inactions in the sense of making excuses to keep yourself safe.

The words you say, the thoughts you think, even the feelings you feel all determine your current reality and the story you keep yourself stuck in.

Nothing is as fearful as being fearless and tenacious because when you are fearless and go after what you truly want, you open yourself up to great change and change is not always comfortable at first.

───── ···❦··· ─────

You can't create great joy, happiness and great success by staying safely within your comfort zone. The magic happens when you take chances and go after your dreams where nothing can hold you back from claiming what your heart desires.

───── ···❦··· ─────

Karma is created by the energetic choices we make each and every day. If you make choices from a place of lack or obligation, you will attract more circumstances that keep you in this energetic vibration. Whereas when you make choices out of joy, freedom or happiness, you'll receive more circumstances within this energetic vibration.

───── ···❦··· ─────

The stories you have been telling yourself over and over again, either attract more of what you desire or blocks the very things your heart desires to find its way to you.

───── ···❦··· ─────

There are no limitations to what you can manifest and create in your life, the only limitations come from you and the illusions that not more is in store for you. Open yourself up to the unlimited resources the Universe would love to bring to you.

———

In order to change your circumstances you must change your story; to change your story you must open yourself up to the reality that you have created for yourself.

———

Who you are today is not who you were yesterday or a year ago. Who you are today is also not who you will be tomorrow, the day after, or years from today, as you grow into a new person each and every day; growing and becoming who you are meant to become.

———

Let go of the past, let go of the worries about the future, be here in the moment because the now is all you have. The now is all that is important.

———

Fear is only an emotion that comes from believes we have ingrained into our consciousness; but the thoughts we had over and over again, which then turned into a belief that is causing us to feel afraid of something to keep us safe from any harm, even if it is only a perceived or imaginary harm.

Emotions is what drive us but behind these emotions lay the beliefs and thoughts we have that cause us to feel a certain way, that causes us to act and behave a certain way and that causes us to make certain decisions and choices that lead us either onto our path or away from it.

The emotional disconnect happens when we allow our ego mind to take control over our every action, emotion, believes and thoughts. To gain back control, go within and allow your true self, your higher self to resurface. Trust that your true self is who you truly are as a divine being.

Your soul communicates with you through your experiences, your emotions, even the circumstances you experience as it attracts these circumstances into your surroundings to get your attention and to guide you. It is your responsibility to tune in and listen for such guidance.

———— ⟶⊙⟵ ————

Never silent your words out of fear that your words are not powerful enough to be heard. Find your voice, speak your truth and share your message as those who are meant to hear your words will listen eagerly.

———— ⟶⊙⟵ ————

There is great wisdom available to you; all you have to do is open yourself up to receiving this great wisdom and follow your internal guidance and intuition.

———— ⟶⊙⟵ ————

Be silent and listen to the silent whisper of your soul as it speaks to you in every moment, giving you the guidance you seek.

———— ⟶⊙⟵ ————

Surround yourself with people who are in alignment with where you want to be, as there is great wisdom to be learned from those who have been on the journey you chose to be on in this moment.

———

The great teachers and mentors of this time enter your life for a specific reason and during a time you are ready to receive their teachings. All happens in divine timing and to your highest and greatest good.

———

In order to change our circumstances we must take responsibility for our choices, the actions we have taken as well as the inactions we took that lead us to experience the circumstances we experience each moment of our life's.

———

We each create our circumstances by the choices we make, the beliefs we have, the emotions we feel and the actions we take. In order to change these circumstances, take responsibility for these circumstances as you are the one who created them consciously or unconsciously.

———

Always stay within your personal power and never allow others to take that power away from you. The only time someone can take this power away from you is when you give your power away.

———— ᴄⱷᴐ ————

Affection cannot be bought, friendships cannot be forced, respect cannot be demanded, you achieve the respect you deserve, receive the affection you desire and build friendships that last by giving yourself the affection you desire first, by respecting yourself first, and by being your own best friend first. All starts with you… the way you treat yourself, the way others will treat you as well.

———— ᴄⱷᴐ ————

No one has power over you unless you give your power away. No one can make you do something you don't want to do unless you allow it, no one can hurt you unless you allow it. Decide on who you want to be, how you want to be treated and be clear on what is simply not acceptable and know that you determine how others treat you by how you treat yourself first.

———— ᴄⱷᴐ ————

Love yourself unconditionally, be mesmerized by your inner and outer beauty and you will radiate this immense and vibrant light that blinds those who have yet seen their own beauty.

———————

Greatness is within you, allow yourself to open up to show the world this immense greatness you hold within, step out from the shadows and shine brightly. You have stayed hidden away for far too long; it is now time for you to step into your true purpose and become the divine being you already are within.

———————

If love is what you seek, give yourself the love you desire from others. The only love you need is the unconditional, unbreakable, wholehearted love you can give yourself. Open your heart to loving yourself unconditionally, even the flaws you feel you have, love those flaws as much as you love the things you already love about yourself, cherish every piece of your physical and divine self. This is where you will find true love, the love for yourself.

———————

It is easy to hide in the shadows of society, to stay hidden and in silence, to not speak your truth as this would make you different. Different from all of those who chose to hide their gifts, to fit within the box of being normal. Embrace your gift of greatness and step outside of the box and lead the way, show others that it is safe to be different, to be more, to do greater things, to have all that your heart desires.

———

Nothing is achieved if you fear to step outside of the shadows of doubt and fear. Break free from those shackles that have held you back for far too long, know that there is magic happening on the other side of the shadows.

———

Miracles happen when you are tenacious enough to step outside of your comfort zone and even if the other side seems frightening, the miracles that await you are worth the risk.

———

Clarity is the essence of manifesting your hearts desire as the universe cannot deliver on unclearness.

———

All that you desire and ask for will appear in your life whenever the time is right. You must open your senses and eyes to the opportunities that appear in front of you to see that the universe has not only heard your asks but also delivers on what you desire.

———— ~⚬⚬~ ————

Be clear on what you desire, know exactly what it is you want to manifest and release your desires as the universe will support you in co-creating the very things you wish for.

———— ~⚬⚬~ ————

The universe is always listening to your wants, desires and even to the things you don't want; it always delivers the very thing you focus on the most.

———— ~⚬⚬~ ————

The vision for how you want to live your life is the first step in creating the very life you desire. Create your dream life in your mind's eye, then hold on to that vision and know that it will unfold in just that way as long as your vision is clear and free of doubt.

———— ~⚬⚬~ ————

Finding clarity and fulfillment in your life starts with finding clarity within; clarity around what you desire to create for yourself, clarity around what is no longer acceptable to you and what you desire instead. Once you have this inner clarity, feeling the fulfillment in life will be within your reach.

———— ·❊· ————

Setting intentions is a powerful way to manifesting your heart's desire but intentions without the inner belief that it is possible, and the conviction within these intentions that you will do whatever it takes and take inspired actions to move towards manifesting your intentions; without all that, your intentions are only words without meaning.

———— ·❊· ————

Miracles can happen all day and every day for those who believe and expect miracles to happen. Open yourself up to the magic and miracles that are all around you, when you believe that miracles are possible for you and you expect them to happen then you will be in awe surprise of what all is truly possible.

———— ·❊· ————

Possibilities are created by your inner willingness to open yourself up to the vast possibilities available to you, by opening yourself up to being, doing and having so much more than you can even imagine. The only one stopping more and greater possibilities to come to you is you alone and your disbelief in the possibilities. Open yourself up and know all that you desire is more than possible.

———————

Surrender your wishes, your desires and wants into the care of the universe and allow yourself to be divinely guided in order to co-create the very things your heart desires.

———————

Clear your mind of the busy chatter as it only distracts you from being present in the now so that you can hear the silent whisper of your soul.

———————

If you are stuck in worrying thinking of the future, dwelling on past experiences, you are missing the beauty of this present moment, the stillness, and wonders that are happening all around you in this present moment.

———————

You don't need to have all the answers as long as you know enough and trust that you are divinely guided, that is enough to move forward on your path. All answers will reveal themselves to you when the time is right.

———————

Allow yourself to enter into the flow of divine guidance as this is where the information you seek will flow freely. Do not force the information as it will block the divine flow.

———————

Surrender to your inner guidance as you already hold all answers you seek within you. Listen to the silent whispers, the gentle nudges of your inner guidance system it is guiding you on your way.

———————

If you feel blocked or disconnected from the divine flow, know that you have the power and choice to go within, to get back into the flow, simply by allowing yourself to listen within rather than listening to your ego mind.

———————

Accept yourself for who you are, and where you are
in life, as you are exactly who you are meant to be and
you are exactly where you are meant to be which is on
your path towards your destiny.

———

Accept those around you as the infinite beings they
are, even if there are people in your life you
disapprove of or judge, know that they are, just like
yourself, part of this world, part of oneness as we are
all one with source, one with god, one with the divine.

———

Acceptance is a choice you can make that will be to
your highest and greatest good, or you can choose to
stay within the energy of judgment, disconnect, and
frustration. The choice is yours and yours alone.

———

Being is a state of allowing, of connectedness, or
feeling part of the great oneness of all.

———

Who you will become is determined by the choices
you make in every waking moment.

———

Becoming is part of your journey that leads you through many life lessons, challenging times, exciting times, as well as situations that mold you into who you are meant to become.

———— ·--~·:·✵✵··~-·- ————

Vision is a clear mental image you create and hold on to in your mind and heart.

———— ·--~·:·✵✵··~-·- ————

Being is a state of being in the moment, where your focus is in this present moment without worries about the future or dwelling on the past. When in the state of being, there is no fear, no worries, no frustration; you simply are connected with who you are within, the infinite being that is part of the greater oneness.

———— ·--~·:·✵✵··~-·- ————

By holding a vision for your life is the stepping stone that leads you towards creating the life you desire. Without a clear vision, you have no clear guidance and you will walk blindly throughout life.

———— ·--~·:·✵✵··~-·- ————

Cherish yourself for who you are, love yourself deeply and unconditionally as this self-love is the purest love you can receive.

———————

We all are unique in our own ways; embrace your uniqueness as it makes you who you truly are. Never be afraid to let others see and experience who you are as anything other than your pure uniqueness would be a lie.

———————

The stories you tell yourself over and over again will eventually turn into your own truth even if they are lies and illusions you kept telling yourself to keep yourself safe and playing small.

———————

You can hide behind the illusions, the lies, and the stories as a means of keeping yourself safe from disappointments, failures, or uncomfortable situations; but these lies and illusion imprison your true self and keeping you from reaching great heights in your life and it is keeping you from away your true path.

———————

Only you know when you are ready but know that your soul has been ready for a very long time and it has been aching to take that leap into your true purpose and go after what your heart desires.

———— ⟶⟨⟩⟵ ————

Your memories of the past are like chapters within a book which can bring you great joy and excitement but also despair and pain. You can choose to skip the chapters that bring you anything other than great joy, happiness, and excitement. You can choose!

———— ⟶⟨⟩⟵ ————

Kindness is an act of love towards yourself and others.

———— ⟶⟨⟩⟵ ————

Any memories of pain, disappointments or fear can be erased by simply making the conscious decision to take back your power, to release the pain as it no longer has control over you unless you allow these memories to keep taking your power away.

———— ⟶⟨⟩⟵ ————

Listen to the truth behind the words you speak. The words you speak may appear as the truth to your ego mind but your heart and soul knows the lies that lay behind these words.

––––––––––

Be true to yourself by speaking words that empower rather than disempower the amazing being you are within.

––––––––––

Your soul only knows truth and love, honor yourself by speaking only words of truth and love as this is who you are within.

––––––––––

Wisdom can be found in every moment, every situation, every word you hear. Open yourself up to receive the wisdom that is all around you as it speaks to you in every moment.

––––––––––

Inspiration comes from the joy and excitement you feel, it is the fuel that drives your actions, that lead you to move forward, towards the destination of your inspiration.

––––––––––

Ground yourself in order to be present in the moment, as in the moment is where the magic and wonders happen.

———— ❦ ————

Share your gift with the world as the world needs all that you have to offer.

———— ❦ ————

Embrace who you are within, do not let the fears, the worries or challenges you may be experiencing hold you back from shining your light and being who you are within.

———— ❦ ————

Value the gifts you have, as they were given to you for a reason but only you will know that reason when you are ready to hear the truth and allow yourself to step into your true purpose.

———— ❦ ————

Others will accept you for who you are if you accept yourself for who you are within and as a whole.

———— ❦ ————

You create freedom in your life and your surroundings by making choices that reflect the energy of freedom.

———————

In order to experience happiness simply choose to feel happy, no matter the circumstances you always have a choice to find and experience happiness in every moment of your life.

———————

The choices we make in every moment creates the life we live. In order to change our life we must change the choices we make into choices that are in alignment with the life we desire to create.

———————

Never turn away the love and affection of others as their love is precious and their desire to give love is just as intense as your desire to receive love.

———————

Your worries and fears can be released as easy as taking off a piece of clothing and putting it away as you no longer need it or it no longer fits.

———————

Your soul is in alignment with your purpose and deepest desires; but are you in alignment with your soul?

———

Your dreams are not as far out of reach as it may seem. Bring in your dreams into your heart; believe that they can be your new reality and take the inspired action to turn your dreams into your new reality.

———

In order to experience great love in your life, let go of the past as it is keeping you from moving forward and from experiencing the deep, unconditional love your heart longs for.

———

Faith comes from a deep inner knowing that all is possible, that there are infinite possibilities and opportunities for great abundance available to you. That inner knowing that knows no bounds.

———

Be open to the wonders of this world, the magic, and miracles that are happening even if you haven't seen them yet. When you open yourself up to the wonders, the magic and miracles this world has to offer, your life will change in an instant.

———————— ⟶•✠•⟵ ————————

Change can happen in an instant if you choose to make choices that are in alignment with who you are within and what you desire to create for yourself.

———————— ⟶•✠•⟵ ————————

The truth is in the moment as nothing else matters; neither the past nor the future matters when you stay within the now as it shows you the truth of this given moment where you are who you are.

———————— ⟶•✠•⟵ ————————

Fears, worries, and challenges are all illusions and lies that aid us in keeping us safe; safe from disappointments, safe from possible failures, safe from uncomfortable situations but it also keeps us safe from growing and becoming who we are meant to become.

———————— ⟶•✠•⟵ ————————

Embrace change as change is where the wonders lay;
its where the magic happens.

———

Feeling uncomfortable about stepping outside of your
comfort zone is a temporary feeling and will soon
subside if you allow yourself to embrace the change
that comes with going after your dreams.

———

Rest and rejuvenate your mind as your soul prepares
itself to step forward and helps you to co-create the
life you desire.

———

The amount of self-worth you feel for, and in
yourself, is the mirror reflection of how you live your
life.

———

There are no benefits in hiding who you are as who
you are is an amazing being that is in this world to
make a difference.

———

All outer experiences are the mirror reflections of your inner self, it shows you the things you dislike about yourself, the things you love about yourself as well as the things you have been ignoring but are beneficial for you to discover.

———

Allow yourself to not only be the change but also shine your light to bring change to those in need.

———

Share your wisdom, share your knowledge, share your love, bring all of who you are to the surface and make the difference you are meant to make.

———

The love for yourself will bring you all the joy, the happiness and success your heart desires. Love yourself deeply and unconditionally and you will feel complete.

———

Those who enter your life may be there to stay or may only be there to teach you something you are meant to learn on your path towards finding and living your true purpose.

———

You'll find peace within when you choose to become one with all.

———

Your inner wisdom will always guide you in the right direction, to make the right choices and to guide you to take actions that are to your highest and greatest good. To hear this guidance focus within as all of your answers come from within.

———

Take action out of inspiration, joy, and happiness as these actions will be in alignment with your true self and to your highest good.

———

Let go of the negativity that is trying to keep a hold on you. You can choose to set yourself free from any darkness and negativity that no longer serves you. You always have a choice!

———

Life is full of choices, what we make out of the moments where we can choose is all up to us.

———

Every day you are presented with opportunities to choose to either continue going down this path or you can choose to change directions and go after the very things your heart desires.

———— ⟶⟞⟝⟶ ————

You always have the freedom to choose; the outcome of your choices will always be your responsibility. If the outcome is not what you desire, decide to choose differently from here on out.

———— ⟶⟞⟝⟶ ————

The freedom you desire can be achieved by taking inspired actions that lead to the creation of the freedom your heart desires.

———— ⟶⟞⟝⟶ ————

The only one that can keep you from experiencing the freedom you desire is you and you alone. Give yourself the permission to be free, to feel abundant, and to experience the things you desire.

———— ⟶⟞⟝⟶ ————

To bring abundance into your life, feel abundant within, notice the abundance all around you as it is already there.

———— ⟶⟞⟝⟶ ————

If you are looking for permission to go after your dreams, never look outside. The permission you are looking for can only be found within. Give yourself the permission you think you need from others. Your own permission is all that matters.

———— ⬥ ————

Never chase after your dreams, instead get into the flow of allowing your dreams to manifest.

———— ⬥ ————

Manifesting is an act of allowing, allowing all that you desire to come to you easily and effortlessly.

———— ⬥ ————

The longing you feel within is your souls' way of whispering into your ear that much more is possible for you and to open yourself up to the infinite possibilities that awaits you once you make the decision to step onto the path of discovering all the possibilities available to you.

———— ⬥ ————

Failure is not to be feared as it will teach you the valuable lessons and it gives you the opportunity to grow.

———— ⬥ ————

The journey of life is an adventure that takes you through many chapters of your life's story. Embrace each chapter as it aids you in getting closer to discovering your true story.

⸻

Success cannot be achieved without the many life lessons we have to experience in order to become the person that allows success into their life.

⸻

Failure is part of success as it will guide you on your path into creating the life you desire.

⸻

Friendships are meant to be nurtured as a nurtured and well taken care of friendship will last beyond time.

⸻

Find joy and excitement in all that you do as this will bring you great happiness.

⸻

Surrendering is an act of allowing for the things you desire to come to you easily and effortlessly.

⁓ ⁓

Share your wisdom, your knowledge, and your message with the world, as there are many who are just waiting to hear your words.

⁓ ⁓

Step out from the shadows and shine your light brightly to bring love and light to the world, to make an impact on those who are in need of your love and light.

⁓ ⁓

You have the immense inner strength to break through the illusions, the challenges, and barriers that appear in your way. Focus on your desired destination and know that you have the inner strength to see things through, no matter how difficult things may appear.

⁓ ⁓

Self-love is an act of unconditional love for yourself, love that holds no judgment, no restrictions or conditions.

⁓ ⁓

Self-love for who you are is the essence of finding
great joy and happiness in life.

———————

Become your own genie by allowing yourself to fulfill
your deepest desires and wishes without any judgment
attached – your wish is your command!

———————

Divinity is the essence of who you are; you are a
divine being that knows no bounds.

———————

The challenges and adversities you are experiencing
are part of your souls path towards finding its
purpose and experiencing life in its human form.

———————

Be present in each moment as this is where you will
experience the freedom of being as there are no fears,
no worries, no doubt. If you allow yourself to be
present in the moment you are free.

———————

The experiences you gain throughout your life are all part of the experiences your soul desires to experience.

———

The wisdom you seek is all around you, it lies within every experience you have, every lesson you learn, every person you meet. Open yourself up to seeing the truth within each experience, each moment, as there is great wisdom to be found.

———

Divine guidance is accessible to you at all times. It comes from the inspiration you receive, the gut feelings you have, even the inner knowing of what to do next or what not to do. You are always divinely guided and never alone.

———

Whenever you come up to a fork in the road, unable to choose what direction to go in, go within and tune into your inner wisdom for the answers you seek.

———

In order to step into the flow of inspiration and divine guidance quite your ego mind to create that inner silence in order to hear the silent whisper of inspiration.

Excitement is the fuel that drives your actions. Inspiration is the actions you choose that lead you towards your desired destination, towards the very things your heart desires.

The excitement you experience is what determines the outcome of the actions you take. Any actions you take without excitement might bring you less desired outcomes. Actions taken with immense excitement will bring you outcomes of much joy and even more excitement.

Be who you are, never hide your true face as your true face is as beautiful as your soul. Be authentic in who you are and never hide.

You can find joy in every moment as it is a choice to feel joy in everything you do.

⸺ ⊶ ⊷ ⸺

You can find that inner peace by accepting that you are right where you are meant to be and that you have the power to create the life you desire.

⸺ ⊶ ⊷ ⸺

The inner knowing of your divinity will allow you to move mountains as it will guide you on your path towards experiencing great joy and happiness in life... if you so choose.

⸺ ⊶ ⊷ ⸺

Accept others for who they are as they too are divine beings on their path to discovering who they truly are. Never judge others if they are different as they are on different paths as you are and they make choices that are to their highest and greatest good.

⸺ ⊶ ⊷ ⸺

When choosing your path, know that the path you choose may change based on the choices you make in every single moment.

⸺ ⊶ ⊷ ⸺

The journey of self-discovery can be a great, fantastic, exciting, but also scary and overwhelming adventure but when you stay your path and not give up you will reach your destination and all the adventures you experienced, both good and bad, will have been well worth it.

Never fear the unknown as it will be uncomfortable only for a moment before great joy and excitement reveals itself.

The joy and happiness you experience in your life is the mirror reflection of the joy and happiness you feel within your heart.

Intention is the key to manifesting your heart's desire as your intentions will set things into motion to bring forth the very things you desire to manifest.

Intentions are powerful as they tell the universe exactly what it is you desire to manifest.

To find inner peace, focus on this moment, go within and quiet your ego mind. Let go of all the worries, the fears, the doubts or needs, simply allow yourself to be. Be present in this given moment and allow yourself to feel the immense inner peace and stillness.

———— ⟡ ————

Indecision is what keeps you stuck; your inability to choose which path to go on out of fear you may choose wrong but know that you can always choose differently and change path. No path is wrong as it all leads you on your way. Trust that you know the answer within.

———— ⟡ ————

When indecision stops you in your tracks, go within, quite your mind and listen to your inner guidance as it will tell you what route to choose. Just trust that you are divinely guided.

———— ⟡ ————

Having a clear vision of where you want to be, what you want to have and what you want to do is the driving force that will help you reach your goals.

———— ⟡ ————

Personal growth is what we seek because only when
our soul can grow, are we moving forward in life.
Without growth, we stay stuck!

———

We each have divine gifts and abilities that were given
to us for a purpose. This purpose may be to help
yourself or it may be of a greater scale to help others
and make a difference in the world.

———

Know yourself as the divine being you are that has
immense powers to manifest the things your heart
desires and to overcome any challenges that may
present itself as a means to lead the way or redirect
you into the right direction.

———

There is no situation, no challenge you cannot master
as you are divinely guided at all times and never alone
on your path.

———

You hold the wisdom within you, all the answers you are looking for you hold within. Your soul has the infinite knowledge you require to master your life and your life's path.

———— ⚬ ————

The lessons we learn, the experiences we gain are all meant to appear in our life as our soul has the desire to experience life, both the good and the bad, what we do with these experiences determine how we live our life.

———— ⚬ ————

To experience freedom we first must free ourselves from the shadows of our past, from the illusions and lies we've been telling ourselves to keep ourselves safe. By letting go of the shadows of the past, the lies, and illusions we ultimately set ourselves free to experience the freedom we desire.

———— ⚬ ————

You can experience freedom anytime you wish by making choices that reflect the freedom you desire.

———— ⚬ ————

The gratitude you feel for what you already have will bring in more that you can be grateful for.

———

Evoke the power of repetition anytime you have an experience you don't want to let go of, an experience that brings you great joy and happiness. Simply ask the universe to bring you more of this experience.

———

By letting go of the old, the energy that no longer serves you, you make room for new and better things to enter into your life.

———

Focus is necessary to complete a task, to keep moving forward as you move towards and through the finish line.

———

Acknowledge where you are now, where you have been, and how far you have come as this acknowledgment will give you the strength to see things through and keep moving forward.

———

Motivation is never far as you can choose to feel motivated, as you can choose to feel excited about where you are heading as this excitement will fuel the motivation to stay on course, to push through any challenges and to move towards your desired destination.

―――――――――

When you feel inspiration never hold back. Share your inspiration with the world, as your inspiration may change someone's life.

―――――――――

The gratitude you feel deep within will magnify and radiate out and bring you great abundance, joy, happiness, and success.

―――――――――

CHAPTER FOUR

THE FIVE STEPS TO MORE JOY, HAPPINESS, AND SUCCESS

The biggest challenge we often face as we are trying to create a better life for ourselves, or create more joy, happiness, and success is the self-sabotaging behavior we fall victim to. We often fear the changes we would like to create because change is uncomfortable, it stretches us and in order to create that change in our life, we have to step outside of our comfort zone which may just be the most challenging step we have to take.

In order to create the life we so desire, there are five essential steps that will help us in taking back the control and claiming what we truly want.

It all starts with *Discovering the Possibilities*! This is your starting point, think about where you are right now, what is your current situation, and then look at where do you rather want to be. What magic would you like to create in your life? What are the possibilities you have right now that you can tap into, what possibilities would you like to have? Also, think about what would you do if you could not fail?

Often times we stay stuck because we are so afraid of failing and all the disappointments that come with failing. But in reality, failing is just another word for feedback. Anytime you "fail" at something you are getting feedback that you can learn from so you know what not to do, or how to change things around so you do it better the next time.

I get it, failing is not a good feeling and often times we take it to heart, we take it personal, we might think we are not good enough because we failed so many times, and that's why we decide not to go down that road again because failure is painful.

But really think about what would you like to create for yourself, what magic would you like to create in your life? What would you do if you would know that you could not fail? What if you would be able to create anything you want, in exactly the way you want to create it; without any problems, challenges or mistakes.

Envision having it in just that way, can you feel the warmth in your chest? Are you getting excited about your vision? Good! Hold on to that! This is the first step in manifesting what you desire.

———— ∞ ————

The second step is **Detecting and Uncreating your Inner Gremlins!** This piece might be a little painful but very necessary in order to let go of your inner gremlins so don't skip this step!

(Please be advised, if you are suffering from depression or any other mental disorder, please consult with your physician first and seek help if needed as this exercise might bring up bad emotions and I would not want anything to happen to you)

In this step you would think about anything you can think of that is holding you back, any events that happened in the past that are still upsetting you. It may even be something that happened to you when you were a small child or a baby. Think of any upsetting moments in your life that when you think about it today still holds a negative charge.

Also, think about how you feel about money, what is your money story and your relationship with money, do you have a good and healthy relationship with money or is it more like a really bad marriage?

I usually don't like to dwell on the past because you can't really change what happened in the past. I rather focus on the future and what I can do today to create a better future for myself and my son; but for this step, I highly suggest to dig deep into your past, uncover anything that you can think of that is still affecting you. Sometimes even the smallest things can have a negative impact on you creating your dream life and business today. The more you can uncover the better!

My suggestion to you is, take some time to yourself, lock yourself in your room or go somewhere where you won't be disturbed and do some soul searching. Take as much time as you need; even take a box of tissues because it can happen that you shed some or a lot of tears, but that is a good thing. If something makes you cry, write it down!

Think of any people who upset you, any relationships that went south, any people who were really mean to you, list everything!

This is step two, digging deep into your past, and also your present and detecting and uncovering any and all of your inner gremlins.

Step three is all about ***Destroying And Uncreating Your Inner Gremlins!*** This is one of my favorite steps because once you got rid of your inner gremlins you will feel like a whole new person, like a heavy weight was lifted off your shoulders.

One thing I do want to mention, this is not a quick fix, especially if you have dealt with your inner gremlins for a long time. They want to come back because you are their home, their mommy or daddy, so be advised that it might take some time to get rid of all of your inner gremlins and some might try to sneak their way back into your life. But the fun part is that you can destroy and uncreate them anytime they come back.

My most favorite technique for getting rid of my inner gremlins is diving into my Akashic Records and healing myself on a soul level but I also use EFT – Emotional Freedom Technique where I release all negative charge around a specific topic and tap in positive affirmation to replace the negative ones.

Another great way of releasing negative energy around different events, and even around people, is to release it into the universe and let it go. I like to say this Ho'oponopono mantra "I Am Sorry, Please Forgive Me, Thank You, I Love You"

Once you release the negative energy and feeling around a particular event or person, you might notice right away how lighter and more relaxed you feel.

You also want to think about what story do you keep telling yourself and to others; are you stuck in a negative story full of lack and negative emotions, or are you telling empowering stories about how great your life is, how successful you are, how great things are going?

Pay attention to what you tell yourself and others and if you notice you are falling into making excuses, playing small because of something you think might happen, ask yourself is this really true or is this just a story you are telling to keep yourself safe and within your comfort zone?

Step three is all about destroying and uncreating your inner gremlins. Do this as often and as much as you need to in order to get rid of your gremlins. Also renounce all ties you have with them, tell them to get out, they are not paying rent, you are evicting them! Out! Out! Out!

Step four is all about *Deciding on Your New and Better Life!*

Now you get to dream big! Think about your goals, your financial goals, your professional goals and also your personal goals. What do you want to accomplish in 12 months, then pick your top three goals and turn them into 90-day blitz goals, and focus on manifesting these goals.

Make an intention for yourself, and for the magic you want to create in your life, write down in as much detail as you can what your dream life would look like, your ideal day, your perfect business/career, write it in as much detail as possible and remember to think of what you want to create for yourself if you know you could not fail.

Also think about your new money story, in step two you defined your current money story, now define your new and better money story. How do you want to feel about money? What relationship do you want to have with money? What would you be doing with all the money you want to have?

Step four is all about dreaming big because you get to create your own future, your dream life, and your destiny. Whatever it is you want to create, you can create but it all starts with knowing what exactly you want to create. The universe doesn't know what you want, it doesn't understand what you mean with "I want a successful business" or "I want to have a better life" or "I want more money". If you are asking for more money the universe will deliver, it might give you $5 which is more money than you have right now. Be as specific and as detailed about what you want to create as you can!

Step five, which is the final step in creating more joy, happiness, and success, is *Designing Your Dream Life!*

Now that you have discovered your possibilities, uncovered and set yourself free from your inner gremlins, and decided on your new and better life, the next step is to turn it into your new reality. Knowing what you want to create is one piece of the puzzle, but to make it a whole picture you need to implement daily practices to make sure you can design this life and business, or career, you dream of.

There are many amazing techniques that you can use and implement and you may have heard of some or all of them and you may have, or still use them. But just as a refresher, here are the strategies I find most beneficial in helping you manifest the things you desire in your life.

The ultimate outcome of all these strategies is to help you raise your vibration, increase your awareness, stay within a positive energy and open the gates to manifesting anything you desire.

So here it goes…. You can use mind movies on a daily basis and turn your vision board into an exciting mind movie with affirmations. You can visualize your goals and how you will feel once you have achieved them. You can meditate, use affirmations, journal, work with a coach or mentor, you can use EFT to continuously tap out the bad and in the good. Or you can get an Akashic Record Consultation to help you heal on a soul level.

Step five is really all about keep raising your vibration and staying within the good and positive vibration in order to attract the things you desire. Anytime you notice falling back into the negative and "icky" vibration, do something to snap yourself out of it, dance, listen to music, watch something funny, do something you enjoy, or pick up this book and read through these messages. If you are receiving the daily emails, and you are using the daily Action Steps then you are working on raising your vibration every day already.

The most important piece to remember in regards to creating more joy, happiness, and success in your life is that you can!

You must believe that anything you want to create in your life is available to you. If you want more joy and happiness, know that you have the inner power to create circumstances that bring you more joy and happiness. If you desire more success in your business or career, then know that you can create that too!

Once you believe that everything your heart desires is already there, that everything you want to create is available to you, you will start to manifest all the things you desire.

Believe with conviction that all that you want in life is already there, that you can have anything you desire because the universe will help you manifest what you want if you clearly ask for what you want if you believe that it will come, and if you are open to receiving it.

If you say, "I really don't know if I can have what I want" then the universe thinks you are not sure about what you want and won't deliver because it won't give you something you don't want or something you are not sure about. I am sure you have heard the saying "Ask and you shall receive"? Well, the universe is listening! If you have wishy-washy wants, you get wishy-washy results. Be clear about what you want to manifest in your life, believe it's possible and be open to receive!

Once you are clear about what you want, focus on taking inspired actions towards reaching your goals, and manifesting what you desire. Trust in yourself, your intuition and don't act out of fear or worries, because acting from a place of fear, or worry, will only push away what you want to manifest and will close the doors on abundance coming into your life.

Sometimes doing less outer work brings more results than trying to force things to come about. The more inner work you can do, the more vibrant you will become and the more of a magnet to what you desire you will become; a magnet to financial abundance, a magnet to more joy and happiness, a magnet to wealth, a magnet to the freedom you so desire.

Go within and see what inner work is required in order to release limiting beliefs, old thought patterns that you are still holding on to. Focus on the now, be open to releasing all the old and negative that no longer serves you and only hinders you from moving forward.

CHAPTER FIVE

A MESSAGE TO YOU

You may think it is difficult, maybe even impossible to create the life you desire, that it takes a lot of hard work and dedication to create this dream life, or that it may not be available to you due to your situation or circumstances.

However, in reality, all it takes is for you to decide that you are ready; to decide to make this dream life of yours, your new reality. To step into your purpose, to step into your power, to trust and belief with conviction that all you desire is truly possible and that it can be your new reality. Know with conviction that you cannot fail because anything you desire is already available to you.

Ask yourself, go within, and be honest with yourself, why have you not claimed this life you dream of yet? It already exists in your mind, now it is time to turn your dream into reality.

Raise your vibration, become your highest, most loving and most vibrant self. Step into the divine, into the infinite white light, raise up, up and up to connect with the higher realms of light. Open your chakras wide, allow the light of the divine to fill your entire body, your mind, your spirit, and your aura. Let it expand wide out. Open your heart, share your love, be open to giving and receiving immense amounts of love and become the amazing light being that you are.

Open your heart to the abundance available to you. See the abundance present in your life, shift into your personal power, be the God or Goddess that you are, the divine being who not only deserves great abundance but who also knows your worth and demands what you desire. Believe that all you desire is yours to have, you do not have to become a different person or learn more skills, all you desire is already available to you.

You are the creator of your abundance! Be open to receiving. Believe that you deserve all that you desire. Open yourself up to seeing all the beauty, the abundance in your life. Know and feel your oneness with the divine, with source, with all that is.

When you let go of your doubts, your fears, and disbelief, you will open up the doors into great abundance, but it starts within you. In your heart you must feel abundant, in your core, you must believe you are abundant.

CHAPTER SIX
FINAL THOUGHTS

I want to thank you for purchasing this book full of inspiration and motivation. These messages are dear to my heart as I feel so very grateful that I was able to share these messages from the Universe with you. I hope these messages have brought you just as much joy as they have brought me. It has been my intention to inspire you that anything is truly possible for you no matter what life situation you are in, or what circumstance you feel are holding you back. I also hope these messages motivated you to let go of your past and to keep moving forward towards creating the life you desire.

I am confident that you will be able to create all that your heart desires and I know this because I have been there, where I barely had enough money to support myself and my son, where I struggled to obtain clients, where I had this deep hunger to make a difference, to help others, but no matter what I did, nothing seemed to be working until I found my way.

Being introduced to the Akashic Records has changed my life. As my mentor taught me the lessons on how to access my own records, to uncover what has been holding me back, and taught me how to heal myself from the shadows of my past, I was finally able to step into my inner power and set myself free from the struggles, the challenges, the worries and the fears. It has opened so many doors for me and I am so very grateful for the guidance I have received to bring these messages to you.

You too have that inner power and the opportunities to make a difference in the world and to create all that you desire. Even if you don't have the ability to access your own Akashic Records, you still have the power to set yourself free from the shadows of your past, from the challenging times and from anything that is holding you back from manifesting your heart's desire. I believe in you!

Because of all that I have learned over the past years, during the challenging times I have experienced and through the breakthroughs I have created in my life, I know that there is light at the end of the tunnel.

If you ever feel like there is no way out, or that things will never change for you, or that no matter how hard you try, things don't seem to be working out for you, know that this is not true! There is always a way! Always light at the end of the tunnel!

Please promise yourself to never give up! Find a way to get inspired, to get motivated to keep moving forward because anything is possible, and all that you desire is more than possible for you.

With deep gratitude,

Kay Sanders

ABOUT THE AUTHOR

Kay Sanders, known as the Creator of Possibilities is an Intuitive Business Coach, Mindset Mentor, Certified Akashic Record Consultant, and Bestselling Author.

Kay helps conscious entrepreneurs find that missing piece to create momentum in their Business and re-ignite their Manifesting Mojo so they can make a difference in the world, create more freedom in their life and tap into the magic and power of manifesting their hearts desire.

Her motto is 'everything is possible' which she also heavily incorporates into her own business and with her clients to help them see all the amazing possibilities life has to offer. Kay truly believes that everyone, not only deserves, but also has the ability, to live a fulfilling life full of success and possibilities.

For more information about Kay Sanders visit
www.KaySanders.com

<u>Also check out her programs:</u>

Manifest Your Heart's Desire – 11 Days To Kick-
start Your Manifesting Power

Mindset Mastery – Design Your Dream Life &
Business

Printed in Great Britain
by Amazon

23692674R00066